GUIDE

TO THE

SCOTTISH PRAYER BOOK

GUIDE

TO THE

SCOTTISH PRAYER BOOK

BY

W. PERRY

D.D. (Aberdeen), D.D. (St Andrews)
Canon of St Mary's Cathedral, Edinburgh

CAMBRIDGE
AT THE UNIVERSITY PRESS
1941

To my Friend

THE RIGHT REVEREND FATHER IN GOD

LOGIE BISHOP OF EDINBURGH

formerly Bishop of Labuan and Sarawak

with thankful memories of his father

J. MYERS DANSON

Dean of Aberdeen

CAMBRIDGE
UNIVERSITY PRESS

University Printing House, Cambridge CB2 8BS, United Kingdom

Cambridge University Press is part of the University of Cambridge.

It furthers the University's mission by disseminating knowledge in the pursuit of education, learning and research at the highest international levels of excellence.

www.cambridge.org
Information on this title: www.cambridge.org/9781107497665

First published 1941
First paperback edition 2015

A catalogue record for this publication is available from the British Library

ISBN 978-1-107-49766-5 Paperback

CONTENTS

NOTE

Since this little book is intended to be a popular guide to the Scottish Prayer Book, it seems best to follow the Contents as printed immediately after the title-page. The reader, however, will find that this method is not strictly logical, as it involves consideration of the Scripture Lessons and Psalter, and the Collects, Epistles, and Gospels before he has studied the services for which these are prescribed. But as the adoption of a different method of treatment would probably result in confusion, we shall explain the services in the order in which they appear in the Prayer Book, and at the same time endeavour to justify the truths embodied in them.

CHAPTER I

Christian Worship and its History

1. INTRODUCTION

WHAT IS WORSHIP? A shortened form of *worthship*, the word means rendering to Almighty God His worth or due. Worship for the Christian is the way of approach to the Divine Majesty. "Going to church" is a phrase which our British reserve has invented to disguise the truth that in worship we go to the throne of grace as creatures to the Creator, as subjects to the King of kings, as children to the Father. Is there any other way by which a living person can draw near to the living God? I know of none. To withdraw from worship is to drift away from God and to serve our own self-made idols. Godlessness is the natural result when an individual or a nation abandons the privilege of worship. When the worth of God is neglected the worth of man declines, until to "fear not God" becomes to "regard not man". Worship is at once the disinfectant and preservative of moral standards.

2. CHRISTIAN WORSHIP SACRAMENTAL

One reason for the ease with which people abandon or neglect the worship of God lies in the fact that there is and must be a very human element in all worship. In itself worship is a spiritual act, yet it can only express itself in human language, human forms, human postures; that is simply because we ourselves are human as well as spiritual beings. Worship, therefore, never can be wholly spiritual; it must manifest itself in outward forms. All worship is sacramental; it has its "outward and visible" form as well as its "inward and spiritual" reality. Outward forms of worship can never fully express the worthship of Almighty God. That is a strong reason not for neglecting the forms but for ensuring that they should be as worthy of their purpose as it is possible to make them. The Scottish Prayer Book, as revised in 1929, is an example of the care which the Church has always taken to refashion and improve its forms of worship from time to time. Neglect of forms renders worship not spiritual but "formless", lacking the "decency and order" which St Paul declares necessary for Christians in their approach to God.

3. St Paul's Principles of Worship

Questions concerned with Christian worship are not settled offhand by quoting the Apostle's declaration, "I will pray with the spirit". He said much more than that. Read I Cor. xiv, 15, 26, 40 and you will see that he laid down four other principles which should govern public worship. Christian worship should be intelligible, edifying, decent or beautiful, and orderly. The first two, intelligibility and edification, have to do with the truth expressed in the outward form; the other two, beauty and order, with the form itself. The crown of all these is the spirituality which is produced by the impact of God's spirit on man's. "I will pray with the spirit, and I will pray with the understanding also: I will sing with the spirit, and I will sing with the understanding also." Yet, "Let all things be done decently and in order", and, "Let all things be done unto edifying".

4. THE STORY OF CHRISTIAN WORSHIP

The long and romantic history of Christian worship cannot be told here. There is room only for a few facts which should be known before we begin to consider the various services in the Scottish Prayer Book.

In early times worship developed freely in different parts of the Church, yet there was always a core which remained the same throughout the Christian world. Down to the beginning of the fourth century the only form of public worship was that for the Eucharist; before that time no other public service was possible, partly because for three hundred years Christians were seldom free from persecution and partly because a large number of them were slaves. The form of service for Holy Communion fell into two parts. The first consisted of Scripture readings, sermon, prayer and praise; this corresponds to our ante-Communion service. The second part began with an offering of the elements of bread and wine and then passed to a thanksgiving to

God, which as early as the third century included the Sursum Corda ("Lift up your hearts") and the Sanctus ("Holy, holy, holy"). The thanksgiving then took up the theme of the Redemption and Sacrifice of Christ and contained a petition, direct or indirect, for the blessing of the elements, after which those present received the consecrated gifts. If you look at the Scottish Liturgy you cannot fail to see this primitive outline embodied there.

5. ENGLISH AND SCOTTISH FORMS

It is a long step to pass from the fourth century to the sixteenth, and one might think that in the course of twelve hundred years changes would be so great that all continuity with the past would be lost. This, however, is not so. Both in England and in Scotland the Catholic type of service for the Eucharist remained substantially the same, as will be shewn later. The first form of service to appear in the English tongue was the Litany in 1544, which was translated from the Latin Litany used in England for centuries before the Reformation. This was followed in 1548 by the publication of a short form of preparation for Holy Communion consisting of "Ye that do truly", the Confession, Absolution, Comfortable Words and the Prayer of Humble Access, which was inserted into the Latin Mass. The first complete English Prayer Book appeared in 1549. The intention of the compilers of that book (with Archbishop Cranmer at their head) was not to abolish the old Latin forms but to adapt these to the needs both of clergy and laity. Before the Reformation the Latin service book took little account of the laity. Even for the clergy it was no easy task to find their way about in the elaborate directions prescribed in these books. The first Prayer Book of 1549 was a masterpiece of liturgical composition; it retained all that was best in the old Latin books and at the same time provided the clergy and laity alike not only with a high standard of worship but also with much more simple forms. In the reign of Edward VI a revised edition of the Prayer Book was published in 1552, most of the changes being for the worse rather than for the better. In the reigns of Queen Elizabeth and James I slight improvements were made.

6. THE SCOTTISH PRAYER BOOKS OF 1637, 1912 AND 1929

It is at this point that Scotland enters into the story. In 1610 Episcopacy was restored to the Scottish Church, and in the reign of Charles I preparations for the restoration of liturgical worship began. These resulted in the publication in 1637 of *The Book of Common Prayer and Administration of the Sacraments for the Use of the Church of Scotland*. The most remarkable feature of that book was its Liturgy or form for the celebration of Holy Communion. In drawing up this service the compilers followed not so much the fourth edition of the English Prayer Book as the much superior edition of 1549, especially in the Prayer of Consecration and the Prayer for the Church. Unfortunately this fine service book appeared to numbers of Scottish people to be imposed upon the Church by royal authority. The public use of it by the Dean of Edinburgh in St Giles' Cathedral on 23 July 1637 was the signal for a riot followed by rebellion, and the Scottish Prayer Book was silenced for nearly a hundred years. The Scottish Bishops in the reign of Charles II made no attempt to introduce the Scottish Prayer Book but were content to put up with an unwritten form which differed little from Presbyterian worship. It was not until the beginning of the eighteenth century that the use of this book was revived, and even then, only at the Holy Communion. The Scottish Communion Office made its way gradually by its manifest superiority to the English; but for all services other than the Eucharist the English Prayer Book of 1662 was universally used. This state of things continued till the beginning of the present century when a desire for more liberty in the use of the English book was increasingly expressed. Modern requirements for a time were satisfied by the publication in 1912 of *The Book of Common Prayer (Scotland)*. This slight revision paved the way for a prolonged examination of all the services of the Church, which resulted in the publication of *The Scottish Book of Common Prayer* in 1929. The preparation for this work officially began in 1918 but preliminary work on the Lectionary and Psalter was going on for some years before that date. In point of fact the Scottish Prayer Book may be said to have taken some twenty years to complete. In their work the Scottish revisers kept in close touch with the authorities of the Church of England, who were engaged in a similar task, and the Scottish Prayer Book owes much to the English Prayer Book of 1928, especially in the revision of the occasional offices of Baptism, Marriage, the Burial of the Dead, etc. Let this chapter end with the judgment of a distinguished scholar on the merits of the Scottish Prayer Book: "The Book as a whole is clearly the best of the Anglican Prayer Books; it draws freely on the rich material provided by the long English debates and is also strongly national, especially as regards the Eucharistic Liturgy and the Calendar" (*Liturgy and Worship*, S.P.C.K. p. 792).

CHAPTER II

Regulation of Worship; Kalendar; Lessons; Psalter

THIS part of the Prayer Book, which is paged with roman numerals, begins with two extracts from the handbook which governs the procedure of the Scottish Church and is known as the Code of Canons (1929).

1. SERVICE BOOKS AND RULES FOR WORSHIP

Canon XXIII states that two Prayer Books are authorized, the Scottish Prayer Book and the English Prayer Book of 1662. You might think that this arrangement would lead to confusion; but the Scottish Church publishes only one book, the Scottish. A few congregations are tied to the English Book by their local deeds of constitution, but these will find in the Scottish Prayer Book the whole substance of the English Book to which they have been accustomed; there is no need to buy the English Book. Canon XXIV, which lays down regulations affecting Divine Service, is interesting. It enjoins that Holy Communion shall be celebrated at least every Lord's Day and on the Great Festivals, when in the opinion of the

Bishop it is "reasonably practicable" to do so. The Lessons may be read either according to the Version of 1611 or according to the Revised Version of 1881, 1884, 1894, but for any change of version the sanction of the Bishop must be obtained. No hymn or collection of hymns to which the Bishop has objected in writing shall be used in any church. Sudden changes in the "customary...conduct of Services" are deprecated; the Rector or Priest-in-charge of a Congregation must "satisfy himself reasonably" that any change made "is not unacceptable" to his people. Bowing at the Name of Jesus is enjoined, especially in the Creeds, and is described as the "customary reverence".

2. THE KALENDAR

Here are set down month by month such Festivals as Christmas and Epiphany (6 January), and the two classes of Saints' Days known as "red letter" and "black letter". Red Letter Days (so called because, in times when printing was cheap, these were printed in red) are those Holy Days and Saints' Days which have a special Collect, Proper Preface, etc.; among them are the Festivals of the Blessed Virgin Mary and the Twelve Apostles. Black Letter Days commemorate later heroes of the Church, such as Ambrose, Augustine, Gregory the Great, and Cyril.

Look at the names in any one month of the Kalendar and you will feel a noble pride at the varied contributions made to the progress of the Church by the Saints from apostolic times down to the year 1380: the martyr spirit, Christian courage, learning, missionary enterprise, personal devotion, and religious community life. You will find in the Kalendar no mention of Lent, Good Friday, Easter, etc.; moveable days and seasons appear in the Tables of Lessons. Before we consider these a few words must first be said about the Christian Year.

3. THE CHRISTIAN YEAR

This venerable institution of the Catholic Church for many centuries has brought before its members in stately cycle the great truths of the Christian faith and the facts on which these are founded. The primary purpose of the Christian Year is to commemorate the events of our Lord's life, His Birth on Christmas Day; His Infancy, Boyhood, and Manhood at Epiphany; His Fast on Ash Wednesday; His Redeeming Passion and Sacrifice in Holy Week and Good Friday; His Resurrection and Ascension at Easter and Ascensiontide; and His Gift of the Spirit on Whitsunday; Trinity closes this first half of the Christian Year with the Christian doctrine of God, which our Lord revealed as the Tri-Unity—Father, Son, and Holy Ghost in one God; the second half of the year is occupied with the work and teaching of our Lord in the days of his flesh. The Christian Year is thus a grand unity. The deepest moods of the human heart are awakened in its course; joy rising up to praise and thanksgiving on the Great

Festivals; sorrow sinking down to the humility of penitence in Lent; the spirit of sacrifice inspired by the Passion of our Lord in Passion-tide and Good Friday; the glory of Christian priesthood by the Ascension, and Heavenly Priesthood of Christ on Ascension Day; the social and family nature of the Christian faith on Whitsunday which celebrates the birthday of the Divine Society to which we belong; perseverance in well doing through the twenty-five weeks of Trinity. Since the Christian Year is a unity, it is foolish to neglect the goodly sorrow of Lent and look for the joy of Easter Day, or to pass by the Commemoration of the Saints and expect to enjoy communion with them.

4. TABLES OF LESSONS

Both the title of this section and the pages themselves look extremely dull. But if you study even a single page with a little care, you will soon find much to interest you. The Tables of Lessons prescribe how the Holy Scriptures are to be read at Mattins and Evensong throughout the year. The Christian Year begins on the First Sunday in Advent, which falls at the end of November or early in December, so that there is a month of one civil year and eleven months of the next in a single Christian Year.

Now look at the Tables and you will see that the course of Scripture Lessons on Sundays is not for one but for three years, marked A, B, and C; if the course of Lessons were drawn up for a single year, the Sunday worshippers would hear only a very small part of the Bible. At the end of the Tables and immediately preceding the Table of Proper Psalms, you will see the years dated; 1941–42 is year A, 1942–43 is year B, and so on, up to 1946–47, which is year C; after this last date, a new Table of Years will be printed. You will not understand the sequence of the Lessons unless you observe that year A continues for twelve months, when year B takes its place, and then year C. In selecting readings the Scottish revisers were guided by such principles as these: suitability for the Christian seasons, Catholic custom, the instruction and edification of the people. It should be remembered that the Bible does not consist of "purple patches", and that a good reader can awaken interest in a passage which may appear to the superficial somewhat difficult.

The Sunday worshipper hears the greater part of the New Testament twice in the course of three years and portions of nearly all the books of the Old Testament and the Apocrypha once a year. For Sunday mornings short Lessons have been chosen in order that the Holy Communion may be celebrated after Mattins within a reasonable time. The week-day course of Lessons, which is for one year, is independent of the Sunday course.

In process of time a dress or array has been developed suitable to the Christian seasons, white for Festivals, violet or purple for Fasts, red for Pentecost and Martyrs, green for the Sundays after Trinity.

There is, however, no hard and fast rule for these colours; the general principle is: the best dress for the highest occasions.

5. TABLE OF PROPER PSALMS

In the Scottish Prayer Book the practice of singing the Psalms according to the day of the month, while it has been retained on week-days, has been abandoned on Sundays and Holy Days, and in the Table of Proper Psalms there is set down a selection for every Sunday and the chief Holy Days of the year as well as for other occasions. It is as necessary to appoint Proper or appropriate Psalms for Sundays and Holy Days as it is to provide appropriate Lessons. The principle followed in this Table has been to select Psalms which in some way tune in with the teaching of the day. On the Sundays after Trinity Psalms not already used have been chosen, and a glance at the Tables shews that these to a large extent cover almost the whole of the Psalter. You should observe that some so-called "imprecatory" (cursing) Psalms have been omitted on Sundays and certain passages from such Psalms are bracketed—not, however, we must admit, with much consistency. Though the Psalms have been the hymn-book of the Church from earliest times, it is impossible literally to turn a Jewish into a Christian book of praise. The genius of the Psalms lies in the fact that they reflect the varying moods of the human heart and that too in a manner that is "naturally Christian". But the Church expects its members to place a Christian interpretation on these Jewish songs, following the example of our Lord, who gave a new interpretation to the Ten Commandments. That is why "Glory be to the Father, and to the Son, and to the Holy Ghost" is sung at the end of each Psalm; the Gloria is intended to baptize the Jewish Psalm into the Christian spirit, and thus in a sense to Christianize the Psalm. In Scotland a distinction is drawn in some quarters between "prose" Psalms and "metrical" Psalms. But it is a complete misnomer to speak of "prose" Psalms. The Psalms as printed in the Prayer Book are closer to their Hebrew form than the so-called "metrical" Psalms of Scottish Presbyterianism; your interest in the Psalms will be much increased if you observe that they are poetic songs, consisting usually of verses, each of two lines, the second of which is a response to the first. Monotony was avoided and variety gained by composers assigning sometimes three lines and less frequently four to a verse. Hebrew as well as Greek and Latin poets had no idea of rhyme at the end of lines in the English way.

If you wish to know the date in any year of Easter, Advent Sunday, Ascension Day, etc. or what the Fasts of the Church are, look at the Tables and Rules printed after the Table of Proper Psalms.

CHAPTER III

The Order for Morning and Evening Prayer; Compline; Litanies; Prayers and Thanksgivings

THE primary object of these services is not the offering of prayer but the singing of the Psalms and the reading of the Scripture Lessons; prayer takes less than a quarter of the time devoted to praise and to Scripture. Mattins and Evensong are therefore better because wider titles for these services; Mattins means what is done in the morning, Evensong what is done in the evening. The object of Mattins and Vespers (Evensong) before the Reformation was to sing the Psalms in course once a week and read the Bible systematically. This practice goes back to the seventh century and indeed may be traced to the worship of the Jewish Synagogue, which consisted of Psalms, Bible readings, a homily or sermon, and prayer. In the Middle Ages, the most important features of Mattins, next to the Psalms and Lessons, were the Venite, Te Deum, and our second Collect; the Benedictus and third Collect came from another early morning service, called Lauds, which was attached to Mattins. Similarly, the Magnificat and the second Collect were distinctive of Vespers, while the Nunc Dimittis and "Lighten our darkness" belonged to a bed-time service called Compline. Thus our Mattins came straight out of two old Latin services, Mattins and Lauds, while Evensong was drawn from Vespers and Compline. The compilation of these two English services was chiefly the work of Archbishop Cranmer, who was gifted with a remarkable power of translating Latin into almost perfect English.

1. MATTINS

Let us now look at the service in the Scottish Prayer Book. It begins with an introductory sentence followed by the exhortation, "Dearly beloved brethren", or an abbreviation of it. The General Confession or a short ancient alternative is then said and one of the two Absolutions pronounced, followed by the Versicles. All this was added to the original form of Mattins which in 1549 began with "O Lord, open thou our lips". The purpose of this addition was to make Mattins a service complete in itself. Note here the introductory sentences for Festivals and other special occasions.

After the Confession and Absolution we are ready to sing God's praise in the Psalms and to hear His word in the Scriptures, the Te Deum preceding the New Testament Lesson and the Benedictus following it. The Benedicite, "O all ye Works of the Lord", and Benedictus Es are recommended for use in Advent and from Septuagesima till Easter, not because they are specially suitable for these seasons but because the

Te Deum comes in with more effect at Christmas and Easter, when it has been omitted for a time before these Festivals. Observe how the Te Deum and Benedicite are now printed so as to shew their structure. The Apostles' Creed is recited at this point, summarizing the Christian faith, portions of which have been heard in the Lessons and Canticles. The ancient salutation, "The Lord be with you", is given to the people, who render the greeting back to the Priest in the words, "And with thy spirit"; "you" and "thy" are emphatic. The Lord's Prayer and Versicles begin the final part of the service which consists of prayer, first in the three collects and then (after the anthem or hymn) in the appointed intercessions. More will be said later of collects and special intercessory prayers.

2. EVENSONG

This service proceeds on the same lines as Mattins, but in our Prayer Book unnecessary repetitions may be easily avoided. The long Confession and Absolution may be said in the morning and the short forms in the evening, or vice versa. Similarly, there is a useful alternative to the prayers after the third Collect as well as a large choice of special prayers printed after the litanies. The Magnificat and Nunc Dimittis, and the second and third Collects, give to Evensong its special character, which is praise allied with quiet confidence and peace.

3. COMPLINE

Compline was the Latin service which completed (hence its name) the seven daily Offices of the Church. It is obviously a late evening service; the opening words strike the appropriate note: "The Lord Almighty grant us a quiet night and a perfect end." The Psalms selected are in harmony with the mood, as are also the Nunc Dimittis, the collect "Lighten our darkness" and the prayers which follow. This simple and beautiful service may not be substituted for Evensong on Sunday but may be used in addition to it. It is particularly suitable as a devotion either before or after a week-night address.

4. QUICUMQUE VULT

This is a canticle rather than a creed, though it is commonly (but wrongly) called the Athanasian Creed. It is pointed as a canticle and in the Scottish Prayer Book it appears in a revised translation under four divisions, the second and third of which are a declaration of the Catholic Faith on the doctrines of the Trinity and the Incarnation. The introductory warning, the theological language, and the length of the canticle at one time aroused a good deal of opposition to its use at Mattins, especially on the Great Festivals; it is now obligatory only on Trinity Sunday, when it may be used either as a creed or as an anthem. The rubric also sanctions its use, either in whole or in part, at other times.

5. THE LITANIES

The length of the Litany in the Prayer Book of 1662 caused that fine supplication to be omitted in many congregations, and the changes made in 1929 were directed to restore this form of responsorial prayer to more general use.

Observe first that the Litany, which is an act both of repentance and of intercession, is printed as it was in 1662 except for certain minor alterations; the unnecessary phrase "miserable sinners" is omitted, "sudden death" is changed to "dying suddenly and unprepared", and certain new petitions for the Ministers of the Crown and for the King's forces have been added; the part beginning "O Lord, deal not with us according to our sins" may be omitted and is printed separately, as in ancient times, when it was a supplication for use in national crises. These changes considerably shorten the Litany. But two "Shorter Litanies" are also provided. The first of these is an abridgement of the above, which reduces its length by a third—and that without loss; this form has the advantage of retaining unchanged the splendid diction of Archbishop Cranmer (the Litany is regarded as his finest composition), and of providing a supplication which can in no way weary the worshipper. The second Shorter Litany is an adaptation of an Eastern form; it is marked by a fine simplicity and is wonderfully comprehensive in the scope of its petitions, though the repetition of "Let us pray" tends to

monotony and the response "Lord, have mercy" is to
the lay mind inappropriate. One of these three litanies
is ordered to be said at least on one Sunday in the
month, as well as on Ash Wednesday and Good Friday,
and is recommended for use at other times.

6. PRAYERS AND THANKSGIVINGS

We now come to a collection of fifty-seven prayers
for a great variety of human needs, and eight thanksgivings for blessings that are common to us all.

An introductory "bidding" (i.e. request) is suggested before each of the prayers, so that the people
may know the object of the prayer beforehand. This
is followed by a versicle and response appropriate to
the purpose of the prayer and is intended to stimulate
and direct the mind of the worshipper. These versicles
and responses may be said by the Priest alone or may
be omitted if necessary, though it is not difficult in
practice to secure the vocal co-operation of the people by
announcing the page. The first prayer on the list is that
entitled "For all Conditions of men". The others are
conveniently arranged under four heads: Seasons, The
Church and Religious Work, The State and the Country,
General. The majority are modern compositions;
yet few, if any, are unworthy of their place beside
such ancient prayers as those "For the Church" and
"For the Unity of all Christian people" (Nos. 11, 12, and
13). The General Thanksgiving takes first place among
the Thanksgivings, which include one "For the Blessings
of Harvest" and another "For Overseas Missions".

CHAPTER IV

The Collects, Epistles, and Gospels; Holy Communion

WE now reach the most important part of the whole Prayer Book, that which contains the Liturgy by means of which the Holy Eucharist is celebrated. This is the highest act of Christian worship and for three hundred years after Christ constituted the sole form of public worship of the early Church.

1. COLLECTS

Only a few notes are possible under this head. The Collects are a wonderful collection of short prayers. The older we grow, the more we admire their simplicity, depth, and rhythm. If you examine a few of them, you will see that they are cast in a certain form and conform to a plan like a poem or a song; that is why they can be intoned or sung with perfect naturalness. Here is the plan exemplified in the Collect for the Thirteenth Sunday after Trinity: (1) The Invocation of God along with the Divine attribute appropriate to the petition: "Almighty and merciful God, of whose only gift it cometh that thy faithful people do unto thee true and laudable service". (2) The petition:

"Grant that we may so faithfully serve thee in this life". (3) The reason for the petition: "that we fail not finally to attain thy heavenly promises". (4) The mediation of our Lord: "through the merits of Jesus Christ our Lord".

The ancient compilers, however, never forced their compositions into the same rigid mould. They omitted the Divine attribute (No. 2) if it did not come naturally to their mind and also the reason for the petition (No. 3) if that might be taken for granted. So you will find much variety of expression in the Collects and at the same time a certain natural fixity of form. As for the content of these beautiful prayers, let it suffice to say that the petitions are invariably for spiritual boons, never for personal or material gifts, though no prayers are more truly personal in the best sense than these Collects.

2. EPISTLES AND GOSPELS

In these is contained the special teaching for every Sunday and Holy Day of the Christian Year. Like the Collects, the Epistles and Gospels were for the most part derived from the pre-Reformation service book. In the Scottish Prayer Book there is provided a number of Epistles and Gospels for such special occasions as the Dedication Festival of a Church and the Transfiguration as well as for the Black Letter Days and week-days in Lent; the translation has also been cautiously revised, "boat" being substituted for "ship", "anxiety" for "care", "robbers" for "thieves", "sign" for "miracle", "body of our low estate" for "vile body", etc.

3. THE HOLY COMMUNION

In the Scottish Prayer Book there are two Liturgies or Communion services, the Scottish Liturgy and the Communion service of 1662 slightly altered and improved. You will note first a page of rubrics applicable to both. The most important of these may be briefly summarized as follows: (1) The Bread for the Holy Communion shall be the purest wheat bread obtainable "whether loaf or wafer" (i.e. unleavened). (2) The mixed Chalice is "customary". (3) Reservation of the sacramental elements is sanctioned "According to long-existing custom in the Scottish Church"; this was a common practice of the Church as early as A.D. 140. (4) Frequent communion is prescribed as a duty.

(1) *The Scottish Liturgy*.

This Liturgy is divided into clearly marked sections so that the worshipper at every stage understands what is being said and done. On so large a subject it is possible to offer the reader only a few brief comments and explanations upon each section.

(a) *The Introduction*. The Holy Table, the Lord's Table and the Altar are all used to describe the place on which the holy Mysteries are celebrated; there is no real difference in meaning between "altar" and "table"; both words are used to describe the same thing in I Cor. ix, 13; x, 21. The word "Presbyter" is used as well as "Priest" to describe the celebrant; there is no difference between the two terms, though in the Authorised Version of the Bible the misleading word "elder" is used for "Presbyter" or "Priest". The Introduction, with the Collect for Purity and the Response to the Commandments, is an act of humble penitence, a fitting approach to the Altar.

(b) *The Ministry of the Word*. This is the title of the second section, which consists of the Epistle and Gospel of the Day (preceded by the Collect) and the Nicene Creed, with the epithet "Holy" restored to the Church in addition to "Catholic and Apostolic"; the word "Holy" was somehow omitted at the Reformation. Should there be a sermon, it will follow the Creed. This section, therefore, is intended for instruction and for the exercise of faith.

(c) *The Offertory*. This was in ancient times an important part of the service. It includes the offering of bread and wine as well as the money gifts of the people. "Blessed be thou" expresses our glad presentation of common material things to the Creator, who condescends to use them as channels of His grace.

(d) *The Consecration*. The call to thanksgiving for these natural gifts is sounded in the Sursum Corda, "Lift up your hearts", and in the Preface, "It is very meet...", ending with Isaiah's hymn in the Sanctus, "Holy, holy, holy". Thanksgiving then passes at once to the theme of Redemption in the opening words of the Prayer of Consecration, "All glory and thanksgiving...". The Words of Institution from the New Testament prepare us for "The Oblation", which means the offering of the holy gifts of bread and wine as the memorial of our Lord's Passion, Death, Resurrection, and Ascension. Then we are ready to invoke the blessing of the Holy Spirit "upon us" as well as upon the gifts of bread and wine; this is done by means of "The Invocation". The great prayer ends (1) with a plea that the Holy Sacrifice thus offered may be accepted for the remission of our sins and the benefits of Christ's Passion; and (2) with a solemn offering of ourselves, our souls and bodies. The note of thanksgiving rings from the beginning to the end of this prayer and the whole prayer is centred upon God, Christ, and the Holy Spirit. This, therefore, is a much richer and fuller Prayer of Consecration than that of the Prayer Book of 1662, which consists only of an introduction, the Gospel narrative of the Institution of the Sacrament and a few lines of prayer between the two. No doubt the Consecration Prayer in the Scottish Liturgy seems to many worshippers unnecessarily long, the more so, since it is immediately followed by the Prayer for the Church, which is also long. But the difficulty of maintaining concentration can be overcome, if the worshipper resists the temptation to wandering thoughts by following the prayer in his book, even though the words may be familiar to him.

The Prayer for the Church is also superior to the similar prayer of 1662, especially in its petition for the departed and its Commemoration of the Saints.

The Lord's Prayer, as in most liturgies, completes the Consecration. The fraction of the consecrated Bread is then made and a brief silence recommended for worship and contemplation. There follows the ancient symbol of brotherhood, which used to be called the Kiss of Peace, "The peace of the Lord be with you all", "Brethren, let us love one another, for love is of God".

(*e*) *Communion*. A more apt title for this section would be "Preparation for Communion", since it includes confession, absolution, and the Prayer of Humble Access. Observe that this section is not broken up as in the English Liturgy, but is a unity as it was originally in 1548.

The Sacrament is then administered to communicants with appropriate words, which being a brief prayer should elicit from each one the ''Amen'' of assent.

(*f*) *Thanksgiving after Communion*. This is introduced by a short bidding or invitation, as in Eastern liturgies, and is followed by a collect of thanksgiving, the ancient hymn, "Glory be to God in the highest", a Post-Communion, and the Blessing.

(2) *The English Liturgy*

"Why", you may ask, "was this Communion service of the Church left much as it was in 1662?" The answer is this. The Scottish revisers agreed that the task of improving the English Communion service was the duty of the Church of England, not that of the Scottish Church. The English revisers, however, took the line of least resistance, leaving the Communion service of 1662 unchanged, and compiling a new form of service as an alternative. Unfortunately the English Prayer Book of 1928–29 was rejected by the House of Commons and therefore technically is not quite legal. The only service book of the Church of England which possesses legal authority is the book of 1662. The Scottish Church could not disown this book which had been authorized for use in Scotland for many years. The English Communion service is, therefore, printed in the Scottish Prayer Book unchanged, save for a few small improvements, such as the permission to substitute the Summary of the Law instead of the Ten Commandments and to use only the first half of the words of administration to communicants. It is, however, worth repeating that the use of wafer bread, the mixed chalice, and the Reservation of the Sacramental elements are sanctioned for the English Liturgy as well as for the Scottish. Those who wish to understand the English Liturgy should read a small book by Dr Lowther Clarke, *The English Liturgy in the Light of the Bible* (S.P.C.K. 1940). For lucidity and scholarship this little book is the best on the subject.

(3) *Appendix*

This section of the Liturgy should not be overlooked. It contains eighteen *Proper Prefaces*, "Proper" meaning appropriate to special occasions; "Prefaces" being introductions to the Consecration Prayer. These strike the note of the Holy Day or season which is observed; the note is struck afresh in the *Post-Communions*, which are Collects that may be said before the Blessing. Nine additional *Collects* are added for use after the Collect of the Day or before the Blessing. The two *Exhortations before the Holy Communion* contain sound teaching expressed in dignified prose. The first of these fell out of use because its warnings against the danger of unworthy Communion went much further than the quotations from St Paul warranted. That fault is now remedied and a note has been added (from the Prayer Book of 1549), urging mutual toleration on the part of those who "use, to their further satisfying, confession to the Priest" and those "that are satisfied with their humble confession to God, and the general Confession to the Church". The second Exhortation is a substitute for the first and is to be used when the Priest sees "the people negligent to come to the Holy Communion". A third *Exhortation at the Holy Communion*, in spite of a strained interpretation of St Paul, is distinguished by an impressive appeal for repentance, charity, and thanksgiving as essential for such as would be "meet partakers of those holy Mysteries".

CHAPTER V

Holy Baptism; Thanksgiving of Women after Child-birth

UNDER these heads are provided the means whereby childhood and youth are dedicated to God. Baptism is the sacrament of regeneration or spiritual birth; the Thanksgiving after Child-birth expresses the natural instinct of the mother.

There are three forms of service for the initiation of persons into the "Body of Christ which is the Church", one in the case of infants, a second for use at private baptism, and a third for the baptism of adults. But as the second is an abbreviation and the third an adaptation of the first, we may confine our remarks in the main to the form for baptizing infants.

1. PUBLIC BAPTISM OF INFANTS

In Scotland the custom of baptizing infants in private houses was fairly common thirty or forty years ago, even among churchpeople, and is still common among Presbyterians. The title of the service now states that the form of Public Baptism is "to be used in the church". Sponsors or godparents must be themselves baptized and, if possible, be also communicants. If such sponsors be not available, the parents of the child may act, and one, in case of necessity, may suffice. The object of these rules is to make sponsorship a reality, and in particular to abolish the unseemly practice of finding at the last moment some casual person to act as a sponsor. You will find the service conveniently divided into six parts:

(a) *Introductory.* This section corresponds to the ancient rite of admitting a learner or catechumen as a candidate for Baptism. It begins with the enquiry, "Hath this child been already baptized, or no?" to exclude the possibility of a repetition of the Sacrament. The Minister then reads a short statement as to the necessity of Baptism and this is followed by one of two prayers, the reading of the Gospel and the explanation attached to it.

(b) *The Promises.* These are prefaced by a short introduction, more simple than that of 1662. Each of the four questions is put "in the name of this child", to shew that the promises are the child's and not the sponsors', who only speak for the child. The Creed, instead of being placed inside a question, is now repeated, as in ancient times, by the Minister and the sponsors. Four short prayers follow, all of them ancient.

(c) *The Blessing of the Water* is now expressed in a much more impressive form than before. It begins with the Salutation followed by the Sursum Corda, then passes into a thanksgiving for the Sacrament of Baptism and ends with a petition for the blessing of the water and a supplication for the grace of the Sacrament.

(d) *The Baptism.* This section contains the central act to which all that goes before has been leading. Dipping or pouring, but not sprinkling, is prescribed in order to preserve the symbolism of baptizing, which implies passing under the water. It is customary to pour the water three times on the child's head; in ancient times trine immersion was of great importance as an outward sign of incorporation into the thrice holy Name—Father, Son, and Holy Ghost.

(e) *The Thanksgiving.* This is introduced by a short bidding to thanksgiving, after which follows the Lord's Prayer. The long prayer of 1662 is now broken into two, the first being a short thanksgiving and the second a petition that the child may be made a partaker of Christ's Resurrection; in this way a much needed simplicity has been gained. This section ends with a new Prayer for the Home of the child, a fitting conclusion to the Thanksgiving.

(f) *The Duties of Godparents.* These appear in our Prayer Book in a more intelligible form than that of 1662 and include a needed reference not only to Confirmation but also that the child may "receive the blessed Sacrament of the Body and Blood of Christ, and go forth into the world to serve God faithfully in the fellowship of his Church". The Duties end with a plea that the sponsors will pray for the child as well as help him to learn and discharge the obligations. A useful rubric states that when Baptism is administered at Mattins or Evensong, the service may be shortened by omitting all the prayers after the third Collect.

2. PRIVATE BAPTISM

This is permitted only when need compels. One or more prayers from the service for Public Baptism are followed by a prayer for the blessing of the water. The child is then baptized and a thanksgiving follows. If no ordained Minister can be procured, then one of those present, male or female, may perform the rite and the words to be used are prescribed. Thus, Lay Baptism, even by a woman, is definitely recognized, though Puritans in the sixteenth century styled the latter "no better than a common washing".

Private Baptism, however, is not in itself complete. It must be followed by the public reception of the child into the Church. The rubric under this form directs the Minister, in the case of a child baptized by any other person than himself, to ask those who bring the child to the church five questions in order to make sure that the Baptism is valid. The service of Reception requires no comment; it is taken from the service of Public Baptism. Note the rubric at the end on Conditional Baptism; if there is doubt as to whether a child has been baptized with water in the Name of the Father, and of the Son, and of the Holy Ghost, the service shall be that of Public Baptism save that at the pouring of water upon the child the Minister shall say, "If thou art not already baptized, *N*. I baptize thee...".

3. ADULT BAPTISM

In the earliest Christian times the service of Baptism was drawn up for adults primarily. Then as the Christian religion spread and Christian parents became numerous, this form of service was adapted for the children of such parents. Down to the year 1662 the only form in use for adults was that for the public baptism of children. In the seventeenth century the extension of English "plantations" in America led to an increase in the number of adult baptisms and the present form was then authorized. It proceeds on the same lines as that for infants, with the appropriate differences that one would expect in the case of grown-up persons. The Bishop must be notified of such a baptism a week before it takes place; instruction in the principles of the Christian religion must be given, and "prayer and fasting" are part of the candidate's preparation for the Sacrament; the candidate must bring at least two witnesses, but these are not sponsors in the popular sense of the word.

4. THE THANKSGIVING OF WOMEN AFTER CHILD-BIRTH

This little office consists of a Psalm, the Lord's Prayer and Versicles, two prayers of thanksgiving, and a blessing. It was originally said before the Eucharist, and this connection is maintained by a rubric which states that if there be a Celebration, it is desirable that the woman should receive the Holy Communion.

CHAPTER VI

Catechism; Confirmation; Holy Matrimony

IN the Prayer Book of 1549 the Catechism was printed within the service of Confirmation, the intention being that the Bishop should examine the candidates on this explanation of the Christian Faith. Hence the Catechism is still described in the title as "an instruction to be learned of every person before he be brought to be confirmed by the Bishop".

1. THE CATECHISM

In spite, however, of the above requirement, the Church Catechism is widely neglected, both in Sunday schools and in the instruction of candidates for Confirmation, on the ground that it is doctrinal and therefore uninteresting. Yet the teaching is simple, the language clear and beautiful, and in the hands of a painstaking teacher the Catechism may be so taught as to arouse and maintain the interest of quite young children.

In its slightly revised form the Catechism is considerably improved; the questions as well as the answers are more direct; brief notes explain the meaning of unfamiliar words such as "hell", "quick", "generally necessary"; the duties to God and neighbour are unmistakably linked with the Ten Commandments. The modest title of the Catechism may be taken to imply that the aim of its compilers in the seventeenth century was to provide only a minimum of Church teaching. No instruction is given on such important truths as the Church and the Ministry, the Holy Scriptures, the Christian Year, and the duties of fasting and almsgiving. The Scottish revisers at one stage of their work made an attempt to supply these omissions but found it impossible to fit brief questions and answers into the frame and diction of the Catechism. A supplementary catechism seems to be the only method of meeting the need of fuller instruction.

2. THE ORDER OF CONFIRMATION

This is now divided into three sections which make it plain that the renewal of baptismal vows is not in itself confirmation, but an edifying preliminary to that apostolic and sacramental rite:

(a) *The Introduction* no longer stresses the baptismal vows but is a true introduction to the service itself. It consists of the narrative of the first confirmation in Acts viii, which clearly indicates that Baptism is not complete without Confirmation; this is also emphasized in the prayer for the sevenfold gift of the Spirit as well as by the sign of the cross.

(b) *The Renewal of Baptismal Vows*. The three vows are no longer put together as a single question. Each vow is taken separately, the vow of renunciation or repentance, the vow of faith ratified by the repetition of the Apostles' Creed by the candidates with the Bishop, and the vow of obedience.

(c) *The Confirmation*, which is the third section, is the heart of the service, and is a complete unity which should not be interrupted by the introduction of any address or hymn. The Versicles, "Our help is in the Name of the Lord..." prepare for the central prayer that the baptized candidates may be strengthened "with the Holy Ghost the Comforter", and daily increase in the seven (i.e. perfect) gifts of grace. This is followed by a little prayer that the outward signing with the cross may be accompanied "by the virtue of the holy cross" and the outward laying on of hands may be the pledge of "the inward unction of the Holy Ghost". The signing with the cross and the laying on of hands follow immediately, along with the short prayer, "Defend, O Lord". It should, however, be understood that the essential confirmation prayer is that for the sevenfold gift of the Spirit and not "Defend, O Lord". The Lord's Prayer and the Collect, with its fine petition that God's fatherly hand may ever be over those on whom the hands of the Bishop have been laid, concludes this section of the service. A final section, bearing the rather obscure title of *The Dismissal*, consists of a prayer for Divine direction and protection, and the Blessing. The pre-Reformation rubric directing that none shall be admitted to Holy Communion until they are "confirmed, or be ready and desirous to be confirmed" is retained. This requires no apology, since Baptism is not complete without Confirmation. The rubric sets up no barrier against Communion (as is sometimes said in Scotland) but simply insists that the privilege of Confirmation is necessary for all communicants.

3. THE SOLEMNIZATION OF MATRIMONY

No service in the Scottish Prayer Book has undergone fewer changes since the Middle Ages than this. A good deal of it may be traced back even to ancient Roman law before the Christian era. That will surprise no one, for a glance at the service shews that it contains the old civil ceremonies of consent and espousal which represent the legal contract involved in marriage. These the Church simply carried over into the Christian service, added the divine blessing, and crowned the ceremony with the Eucharist. In the Middle Ages, therefore, the substance of the service consisted of the espousals or promises, a twofold blessing, and the nuptial Mass. All this has been retained in the Scottish Prayer Book. The title of the service is followed by an important canon, forbidding the clergy to marry persons within the forbidden degrees (e.g. a deceased wife's sister) and parties to a divorce.

(*a*) *The Introduction* is a statement upon the high estate and dignity of Christian marriage, which "was ordained. . .that children might be brought up in the fear and nurture of the Lord" and also "for the mutual society, help, and comfort that the one ought to have of the other". This is followed by a solemn warning to the bride and bridegroom that, if there be any known impediment to the marriage, it should be now declared. The warning, which is pre-Reformation, shews how careful the Church has been to ensure that there shall be no doubt as to the validity of a Christian marriage. The next section bears the title of

(*b*) *The Marriage.* The Priest questions the man and the woman in the same terms as to their willingness "to live together after God's ordinance in the holy estate of Matrimony. . .so long as ye both shall live". The woman is then given to be married by a relative or accredited person—a caution against a forced or clandestine marriage—and the marriage vows are pledged "till death us do part". Thus the lifelong character of the marriage is unmistakable; the marriage in church of a divorcee would be a mockery of the Prayer Book service. The ceremony of the ring also emphasizes the lifelong pledge of fidelity; the ring is blessed by the Priest and the declaration of the man that he shares with the woman all his worldly goods is made. A prayer of blessing precedes the formal declaration of the marriage and the first blessing of the married couple is given.

(*c*) *The Benediction* is the title of the third section, which includes a Psalm to be sung or said in procession to the Altar, the Lord's Prayer, Versicles and three other prayers, and ends with the second blessing. A final rubric continues the ancient practice known as the Nuptial Mass (Holy Communion), for which a special Collect, Epistle, and Gospel are provided. There is also *A Form of Benediction of Married Persons*, that is, of persons married by a civil ceremony; this is derived from the service already described.

CHAPTER VII

Visitation and Communion of the Sick; Burial of the Dead; A Penitential Service

NOWHERE in the Gospels do we find our Lord regarding sickness and disease as judgments of God, still less as punishments for sin. Nowhere does He lend countenance to the not uncommon idea that mere submission is the right attitude to suffering. On the contrary, He treats the grim realities of disease and pain as forces which should be resisted and if possible overcome. His mission and the mission He bestowed upon His Apostles was to heal the sick. It is therefore strange that the old Jewish conception of suffering as a judgment or punishment should have persisted even into comparatively recent times. In the Middle Ages, though the prospect of recovery from sickness was not forgotten, the services of the Church were arranged in a sequence that moved from the sick bed to the grave. The Visitation of the Sick was followed by an examination of the sufferer in faith and repentance; his confession was made and absolution pronounced. This led on to Extreme Unction (anointing with oil) and the Viaticum or Holy Communion, rites which were administered only when the sick person was at the point of death. It is on this account that in the Prayer Book of 1662 the office of the Visitation of the Sick was coloured by a sombre conception of suffering and disease.

1. The Visitation of the Sick

In the Scottish form the whole tone of the service is altered; restoration to health is the plea of the prayers and hope is the spirit in which they are expressed.

The connection, however, between the ancient rites for the sick and our present forms is still maintained in the sections into which the Visitation of the Sick is divided.

(a) *The Visitation* is the first of these. It begins with the fine old salutation "Peace be to this house, and to all that dwell in it", and includes the Kyries, the Lord's Prayer and Versicles. Five short prayers follow, the first being the ancient prayer for recovery and the other four admirable adaptations of a former gloomy prayer which was calculated to encourage neither hope nor cheerfulness in the sick person. Two depressing exhortations in the Prayer Book of 1662 are now omitted.

(b) *Faith and Prayer* is the title of the second section. Instruction is to be given and prayer enjoined that the "days of sickness may be a time of faithful and loving intercourse with God".

(*c*) *Repentance*. Under this heading is included the duty of self-examination and a form of private confession and absolution, if the sick person "feel his conscience troubled with any weighty matter". The ancient prayer which follows is a prayer for pardon, because forgiveness is bestowed not through the formal declaration alone, "I absolve thee", but in answer to prayer.

(*d*) This section contains the rites of *Anointing, and Laying on of Hands* which have Scriptural warrant (St James v, 14; St Mark vi, 5 and xvi, 18). The old Antiphon "O Saviour of the world" precedes and follows the 23rd or other Psalms, and the formula "I anoint thee" is succeeded by a short prayer for "perfect restoration to health". Similarly, the laying on of hands is accompanied by prayer and the Aaronic blessing. A final section contains special prayers for healing, for one troubled in conscience, for a convalescent, for a sick child, and for the dying, and ends with the moving farewell in the name of the Trinity and in communion with the Saints and Angels, taken from the Latin service, "Go forth upon thy journey, from this world, O Christian soul, In the Name of God the Father.... May thy portion this day be in peace, and thy dwelling in the heavenly Jerusalem. Amen."

2. THE COMMUNION OF THE SICK

There are two methods of receiving the Holy Communion in sickness, the first by means of a Celebration in the house, the second with the "Reserved Sacrament", that is, with the holy Gifts consecrated at a Celebration in church, a portion of which have been "reserved" for communicating the sick; the latter is the ancient practice, for it is mentioned as customary as early as Justin Martyr (A.D. 140). Moreover, Reservation involves less strain upon the sick person, and enables him to realize the social nature of the Sacrament and his fellowship with the congregation to which he belongs. This practice is also more convenient for the clergy, especially at the Great Festivals when a priest may expect to communicate as many as four or five in a single morning. Forms are provided for both methods of administering the Holy Sacrament. Note that the ancient rubric on spiritual Communion (when the sick person is physically incapable of receiving the sacramental elements) has been retained. "Only believe and thou hast eaten" was the phrase in which this spiritual act was expressed in the Latin book.

3. THE BURIAL OF THE DEAD

Throughout the ages the Church has been as tender in her concern for the departed and those who mourn their loss as she has been in her care for the sick and afflicted. Before the Reformation there were three rites for the burial of the dead: (1) the morning and evening offices known as Mattins and Vespers into which were inserted appropriate Psalms and antiphons, (2) the "Requiem Mass", which was the Eucharist directed to the departed by means of special prayers and the antiphon "Eternal rest grant unto them" and (3) the interment, which was a short Office at the grave.

The Burial service of 1662 was a poor adaptation of this, cold almost to the point of heartlessness, with a vague remembrance of, rather than direct prayer for, the departed; there was no prayer for mourners and no choice of lessons; the service was compiled for the edification of the living rather than for the peace of the departed and the comfort of the mourners; it therefore lacked the mingled hope and sympathy which should be the Christian attitude to death and the future life. All this is changed in the Scottish Prayer Book not so much by omission from the former service as by additions to it. *The Procession* is a good title which explains the opening sentences, now supplemented and enriched. *The Service in Church* corresponds to the old Office for the departed; it consists of a selection of Psalms, lessons and prayers according to the discretion of the Minister; the Gloria at the Psalms may be replaced by the ancient prayer "Rest eternal grant unto them". A large (perhaps too large) choice of prayers is given, including one for mourners and several for the departed. *The Burial* contains a commendation of the soul of the departed to God as well as of his body to the ground, and the mistranslation "vile body" is changed to "the body of our low estate". Provision is also made for cremation and for burial at sea.

The Communion corresponds to the old Requiem Mass and a rubric states that "It is desirable...to have a celebration of Holy Communion" with the special Collect, Epistle, and Gospel appointed. There is also a prayer for the *Benediction of a Grave in Unconsecrated Ground*.

The Burial of Baptized Children has been framed on the same lines and is tenderly appropriate in the case of a young child.

4. A PENITENTIAL SERVICE

This has taken the place of "A Commination, or Denouncing of God's anger and judgements against sinners"—a somewhat forbidding title. In the Prayer Book of 1662 the "sentences of God's cursing against impenitent sinners" were drawn chiefly from the Old Testament and were misunderstood by the ordinary worshipper. These are omitted from the present Penitential Service and the Ten Commandments substituted. The result, however, is not satisfactory. Fortunately, the latter part of the service remains unchanged, a devout and moving act of repentance, suitable for Ash Wednesday and other occasions.

CHAPTER VIII

Ordination Services and
the Accession Service

1. THE ORDINAL

THE services for the three Orders of the ministry are distinguished in their titles thus: The Making of Deacons, The Ordering of Priests, and The Consecration of Bishops. But there is no real difference between "making", "ordering", and "consecration"; all three are in Holy Orders; the difference of terms merely distinguishes the ascending grades of office. The Preface to the Ordinal is important as shewing the resolve of the Church to continue the Catholic ministry. It states that the three Orders are "continued" as Scriptural and primitive; in other words, the Reformers had no intention of setting up a new Church. This is confirmed by the further statement that none shall be "accounted or taken to be a lawful Bishop, Priest, or Deacon" unless he has had "Episcopal Consecration or Ordination". Apostolic Succession is a fact of "Holy Scripture and ancient Authors"; "from the Apostles' time there have been these Orders of Ministers in Christ's Church; Bishops, Priests, and Deacons".

The three forms of service are framed on the same

lines and are inserted, as in the earliest times, within the Eucharist. Naturally the Ordination to the Priesthood is a richer and more solemn rite than the Making of a Deacon, while the Consecration of a Bishop is of a still higher order. When Deacons and Priests are ordained at the same time, the service may appear complicated, but the difficulty in following it is more apparent than real, especially if one remembers that the Ordination service proceeds within the Eucharist.

The essence of ordination both in Scripture and in the primitive Church was prayer and the laying on of hands. But though this was continued in the Latin books known as Pontificals, it was obscured by ceremonies, quite edifying in themselves but misleading when assigned an importance to which they were not entitled. Hence arose the mischievous idea that the significant moment at the ordination of a Priest occurred when he was given a paten and chalice as a badge of his office, with the formula "Receive power to offer sacrifice both for quick and dead". Not many years ago a Scottish Bishop publicly declared that the words in our Prayer Book, "Receive the Holy Ghost. Whose sins thou dost forgive, they are forgiven...", were essential to the ordination of a Priest, and was astonished when informed that on his theory no Priests were validly ordained until the Middle Ages, when these words were introduced.

The principal features of the Ordination services are the presentation of the ordinands to, and their examination by, the Bishop, prayer that they may faithfully fulfil their ministry, and the laying on of hands; the formula "Receive the Holy Ghost for the Office and work of a Priest (or Bishop)" is an impressive and appropriate addition.

2. THE ACCESSION SERVICE

This contains forms of prayer with thanksgiving for use upon the anniversary of the day of the Accession of the Reigning Sovereign. It was authorized in the reign of Queen Elizabeth by royal and national rather than by ecclesiastical authority; probably for this reason the service has never come into regular use, though it has been printed in the Prayer Book since the sixteenth century and has undergone considerable improvements since that time. Obviously, the anniversary of the accession of the sovereign to the throne is intended to be a day of national thanksgiving. It may be used not only on the day itself but also upon the Sunday before or after it, if so appointed by authority. Congregations would greatly appreciate the service if they had the opportunity of taking part in it.

There are three forms of prayer: the first prescribes special Psalms and Lessons for Mattins and Evensong, special suffrages after the Creed, a collect after the first Collect of the Day and three prayers after the Litany or the third Collect; the last of these prayers is a fine prayer for unity. At the Holy Communion a Collect, Epistle, and Gospel are provided. There is also a third form which may be used on the same day or at any convenient time; this contains the Te Deum, suffrages, and the prayers above mentioned, and might well be used after the third Collect at Evensong on any important national occasion.

CHAPTER IX

"*The Best of Anglican Prayer Books*"

THIS is the verdict on the Scottish Prayer Book of a distinguished scholar, who has examined all the revised Prayer Books in the Anglican communion; those used in the Churches of the United States, Ireland, South Africa, Canada, Ceylon, as well as the Prayer Book of 1928 endorsed by the National Assembly and the Convocations of the Church of England. Can this judgment be accepted and, if so, on what grounds? In other words, what are the distinctive merits of the Scottish Book of Common Prayer?

1. SIMPLICITY

If Prayer is to be "Common" in the sense that a whole congregation can intelligently participate in it, pains must be taken to ensure simplicity both in the order, the thought, and the language of the services. Further, the services ought to be set forth in such a way that the laity have no difficulty in "finding the place". Take this last point first. In the cheaper copies of the Prayer Book you will see on the inside cover a page of clear and simple directions about the order of each service; these are helpful, especially to those in Scotland who may be unfamiliar with a service book. Again, the large number of special intercessions and prayers printed after the Litany may at first puzzle such a person. But if he will note that the prayers are grouped under appropriate headings, he will find his bewilderment gone. Thus, if intercession for Missions Overseas be announced, he will turn to the heading "The Church and Religious Work"; if the subject is the Unity of the British Empire, he will look for the heading "The State and the Country", and so on. Simplicity is also gained by printing all matter which is used only occasionally, at the end of the service to which it belongs, so that people are not confused by having to skip pages applicable only to Holy Days or special occasions.

Further, it is important to indicate in some degree the march of the various services, and this is done most effectively by dividing each one into sections with suitable titles. In the case of Mattins and Evensong, however, this is not possible because these Offices are devoid of a definite climax. But at the Eucharist, at Holy Baptism, and at Confirmation the central point is obvious and it is easy to assign to different parts of each of these services intelligible titles.

Finally, the substitution of modern for archaic terms and the explanation of misleading words also make for simplicity. Examples of the former are "manner of life" for "conversation", "living" for "lively", "honour" for "worship" (in the marriage service), "desires" for "lusts". Explanatory footnotes make clear the meaning of such words as "hell" in the Apostles' Creed and "generally" in the Catechism.

2. CATHOLICITY

Dignity and reverence, however, must not be sacrificed to simplicity, and in public worship these qualities are best ensured by careful attention to Catholic precedent and practice. The golden age of Christian worship lies in the fourth, fifth, and sixth centuries rather than in the twentieth, just as the golden age of church architecture is to be found in the period from the twelfth to the sixteenth century. Ancient liturgies and collects are prized not because they are ancient but because they are infinitely better than modern ones. Again, the Scottish Liturgy is superior in dignity to the English in its tone of thanksgiving, in its theology of the Holy Spirit (who receives no mention in the English Consecration Prayer) and in the logical arrangement of its various parts; and its impressiveness is due to the fact that it owes much to the liturgies of the Eastern Church. On the other hand, the increased number of Proper Prefaces for such holy seasons as Advent or Lent and for such days as Festivals of the Epiphany and All Saints was suggested by Western liturgies of early times. Other examples of the Catholicity of the Prayer Book are to be seen in the enlargement of the Kalendar and in the introduction

61

of Sursum Corda (with its call to thanksgiving) into the Baptismal and Ordination services.

3. FREEDOM

No Anglican Prayer Book is so practical in its sympathy with the requirements of the present day as the Scottish. This comes out especially in the Table of Proper Psalms, in the choice and shortening of the Lessons on Sundays at Mattins and Evensong, and in its use of the Athanasian Creed. The Scottish Prayer Book is liberal in the best sense of the word. On a Great Festival when Mattins is followed by the Holy Eucharist it is not necessary to confess our sins twice or to recite two creeds; permission is therefore given to begin Mattins at "O Lord, open thou our lips" and pass to the Eucharist after the Benedictus. Our enlarged freedom finds expression in many other ways. At the Eucharist the Nicene Creed, the Comfortable Words and the Gloria in Excelsis may be omitted on week-days and one of the three Litanies may be used at Evensong as well as at Mattins. The Christian doctrine of sin, our Lord's attitude to sickness and suffering, and the Catholic conception of the future life are now better understood than was possible even thirty years ago and, as a consequence, the Ministration of Baptism, the Visitation of the Sick, and the Burial of the Dead have been given a much more Christian spirit. The Tables of Lessons also shew that care has been taken to recognize the results of modern criticism of the Old Testament and many inaccuracies in the translation of the Epistles and Gospels have been removed.

4. SPIRITUALITY

"God is a Spirit: and they that worship him must worship him in spirit and in truth." That is the supreme purpose of all liturgies, but to describe how this purpose is achieved in the Scottish Prayer Book would require a volume. Let it suffice to say that the history of the Church would be meaningless if we were to doubt that, where the Prayer Book is faithfully used, men and women are raised from natural to spiritual altitudes, from earth to heaven, from self-absorption to God. But spiritual things must be "spiritually discerned" and the Prayer Book is a spiritual thing which demands time and perseverance as well as faith for its appreciation. Its services were not compiled for the spasmodic worshipper who attends his church once a month or even once a week. On the contrary it assumes that the Holy Communion will be celebrated at least every Sunday and Holy Day, and Mattins and Evensong sung or said every day. Only when we have persevered in this high standard of worship can we expect to discern the full spiritual value of the Prayer Book and to enjoy the treasures within its covers which have enriched the souls of the faithful from one generation to another.

Lightning Source UK Ltd.
Milton Keynes UK
UKHW022012310820
369016UK00019B/499

9 781107 497665